A Tech Incubator For Today

Paramendra Kumar Bhagat

Book Outline: *A Tech Incubator for Today*

Introduction: The New Age of Entrepreneurship (Page 6)

- Overview of the transformative potential of technology today
- The shift from the early days of the internet to the present era
- The purpose of the book: inspiring bold, innovative entrepreneurship

---

Chapter 1: Lessons from the Past (Page 10)

- The rise of the internet and early tech pioneers
- Key lessons from the successes and failures of past decades
- How these lessons apply to today's entrepreneurs

Chapter 2: The Convergence of Technologies (Page 16)

- Exploration of the 10 "internet-sized" technologies shaping the future
    - AI, blockchain, biotechnology, renewable energy, etc.
- The power of intersection: what happens when technologies converge
- Examples of companies thriving at the intersections

Chapter 3: The Bold New Era of Innovation (Page 22)

- Why today is the most exciting time to be a tech entrepreneur
- The abundance of tools, resources, and opportunities available now

- How to cultivate a bold mindset

Chapter 4: The Global Entrepreneur (Page 29)

- The shift from local to global entrepreneurship
- Breaking geographical barriers in talent, capital, and markets
- Strategies for building globally impactful companies

Chapter 5: Tackling Big, Bad Problems (Page 36)

- Identifying "big, bad problems" worth solving
- The societal, environmental, and economic challenges that need attention
- How to frame bold ideas as actionable business opportunities

Chapter 6: Designing the Modern Tech Incubator (Page 44)

- What a tech incubator must look like in today's era
  - Global networks, digital tools, diverse talent pools
- The importance of support systems for startups
- Case studies of successful modern incubators

Chapter 7: From Vision to Reality (Page 52)

- Turning big ideas into executable plans
- Building strong teams and aligning them with a shared vision
- Funding, scaling, and navigating the startup lifecycle

Chapter 8: Thriving in the Age of Abundance (Page 60)

- Understanding the concept of the *Age of Abundance*
- How tech entrepreneurship is enabling abundance at scale
- Practical steps for entrepreneurs to contribute to this vision

Chapter 9: The Role of Capital in the Global Tech Ecosystem (Page 69)

- The evolving role of venture capital and funding sources
- Why access to capital is no longer a limiting factor
- Strategies for attracting investors in the new global economy

Chapter 10: The Future of Tech Entrepreneurship (Page 77)

- Predictions for the next 10 years of innovation
- Industries poised for disruption and growth
- Inspiring entrepreneurs to seize opportunities and make a difference

Conclusion: The Call to Boldness (Page 86)

- Reiterating the need for courage and vision in entrepreneurship
- Encouraging readers to embrace challenges and create meaningful impact
- Closing thoughts on the legacy of tech entrepreneurs in shaping the future

Introduction: The New Age of Entrepreneurship

When the internet burst onto the scene and entered mainstream consciousness, it heralded a revolution unlike anything humanity had seen before. The world, previously constrained by the physical boundaries of communication and commerce, was suddenly transformed into a connected ecosystem where ideas, businesses, and innovations could travel at the speed of light. The energy of that era was palpable—something profound was happening. It felt as though the very fabric of society was being rewoven, and for those at the forefront, the possibilities seemed limitless.

The rise of the internet marked the beginning of an unprecedented technological era. It was a time when young entrepreneurs could dream of building global empires from their garages, a time when the barriers to entry into business were shattered, and a new digital economy was born. Companies like Amazon, Google, and Facebook not only emerged but reshaped entire industries, from retail to information and communication. Yet, for all its transformative power, the internet was just the beginning. The foundations laid during those early years have now given rise to a new wave of innovation that is redefining what is possible.

Thirty years later, the story is no longer about just one groundbreaking technology—it's about the convergence of many. Artificial intelligence (AI), biotechnology, blockchain, quantum computing, renewable energy, robotics, and space exploration are just a few of the fields that are advancing at an extraordinary pace. Each of these technologies, in isolation, has the potential to change the world. But the real magic happens when they intersect—when AI accelerates breakthroughs in medicine, or blockchain transforms global finance. These intersections are creating possibilities that are difficult to fathom, let alone predict.

This convergence has ushered in what many are calling a second renaissance of innovation. While the early days of the internet felt groundbreaking, the era we are entering now has the potential to be even more transformative. The technologies we are developing are not just tools for communication or commerce; they are redefining what it means to be human. Consider the implications of gene editing through CRISPR, or the ability of AI to diagnose diseases with greater accuracy than human doctors. These advancements have the potential to extend life expectancy, eradicate diseases, and fundamentally change the way we live, work, and interact.

For entrepreneurs, this is the most exciting time in history. The barriers that once limited innovation—access to information, capital, and talent—are dissolving. Knowledge is now globally distributed, thanks to the internet and open-source platforms. Crowdfunding and decentralized finance are opening new avenues for capital, and the democratization of education through platforms like Coursera and Khan Academy is creating a global talent pool. Entrepreneurs today have access to tools and resources that would have been unimaginable even a decade ago.

But this also means the stakes are higher. The problems we face today—climate change, resource scarcity, global health crises, and economic inequality—are more complex and interconnected than ever before. These are not issues that can be solved with incremental improvements or simple solutions. They require bold thinking, innovative approaches, and a willingness to tackle challenges head-on. Entrepreneurs who rise to the occasion, who are unafraid to confront these "big, bad problems," have the opportunity to make an outsized impact.

This new age of entrepreneurship is also defined by its global nature. In the early days of Silicon Valley, innovation was localized. The best and brightest flocked to a small geographic area, creating a hub of talent, capital, and ideas. But today, innovation is everywhere. The rise of remote work, digital collaboration tools, and a globalized economy means that a groundbreaking startup can emerge from Nairobi as easily as it can from Palo Alto. Talent is no longer constrained by geography, and neither is opportunity.

This global perspective is not just a matter of inclusivity; it is a competitive advantage. The best ideas often come from diverse perspectives, and entrepreneurs who embrace this global mindset are better positioned to create solutions that resonate on a worldwide scale. At the same time, access to global markets means that even small startups can think big, reaching customers across continents and scaling faster than ever before.

The role of the entrepreneur in this era is not just to create wealth but to solve meaningful problems. The traditional narrative of entrepreneurship—of building a company, scaling it, and exiting with a profit—feels increasingly outdated in a world where the stakes are so high. The new generation of entrepreneurs is motivated by a sense of purpose. They see their work not just as a business but as a form of service, leveraging technology to address humanity's greatest challenges.

This is where the concept of the *Age of Abundance* comes into play. Prophecies and visions of abundance have existed in human imagination for centuries, but for the first time, they are within reach. Technologies like AI and renewable energy are not just solving problems; they are creating opportunities to generate abundance in ways that were once unimaginable. Energy, food, education, and healthcare—areas that have traditionally been defined by scarcity—are being redefined by technology. Solar power, vertical farming, and telemedicine are just a few examples of how technology is making essential resources more accessible and affordable.

Entrepreneurship in this context is not just about building companies; it is about shaping the future. Entrepreneurs today are architects of the world we will live in tomorrow. Their work will determine whether we can overcome the challenges we face and realize the potential of the technologies at our disposal.

This book is a call to boldness. It is a manifesto for the entrepreneurs who are ready to step into this moment with courage, creativity, and a sense of purpose. It is for those who are unafraid to take risks, to think big, and to tackle the problems that others deem unsolvable. It is a roadmap for navigating the complexities of the modern entrepreneurial landscape, from understanding the convergence of technologies to building globally impactful companies.

The journey ahead is not for the faint of heart. It requires resilience, adaptability, and an unwavering belief in the power of innovation to create a better future. But for those who are willing to take the leap, the rewards—both personal and societal—are immense. The tools are in place, the opportunities are endless, and the world is waiting for the next wave of transformative ideas.

The real action is now. This is the moment for entrepreneurs to rise to the occasion, to embrace the challenges of our time, and to build the future we all hope to see. Let us begin.

Chapter 1: Lessons from the Past

The story of technological innovation is as old as human civilization. From the wheel to the printing press to the steam engine, each new breakthrough has not only transformed society but also created ripple effects that have shaped the course of history. However, the pace of innovation has accelerated dramatically in recent decades, thanks to the advent of the internet. As we enter a new age of entrepreneurship, it is worth reflecting on the lessons of the past—the successes, the failures, and the pivotal moments that have brought us to where we are today.

The Early Days of the Internet

When the internet emerged as a commercial technology in the 1990s, it was akin to the discovery of a new continent. Suddenly, there was a vast, uncharted frontier filled with opportunities for those daring enough to explore it. Early pioneers like Amazon, eBay, and Yahoo! led the charge, creating entirely new ways for people to shop, connect, and find information. These companies were not just businesses; they were experiments in what the internet could become.

One of the key lessons from this era is the power of timing. Many ideas that succeeded during the dot-com boom were not inherently unique—online retail, social networking, and search engines had been conceptualized before. What set the winners apart was their ability to execute at the right moment. Amazon, for example, capitalized on the growing popularity of online shopping, a concept that would have been difficult to scale even a few years earlier when internet adoption rates were lower.

Timing is as much about readiness as it is about vision. Many companies during the dot-com boom failed not because their ideas were flawed but because they were too early. Webvan, an online grocery delivery service, had an innovative concept but collapsed under the weight of its own ambition. Infrastructure like high-speed internet and the widespread adoption of smartphones—both critical for online delivery models—were not yet in place. The lesson is clear: being ahead of your time can be as perilous as being behind it.

The Importance of Adaptability

Another crucial takeaway from the early days of the internet is the importance of adaptability. In a rapidly changing technological landscape, companies that fail to evolve often fade into obscurity. Consider MySpace, once the dominant social networking platform. Despite its early success, it failed to innovate at the same pace as its competitors, particularly Facebook. While Facebook continually refined its user experience and expanded its ecosystem, MySpace stagnated, eventually losing its relevance.

The same lesson applies to entrepreneurs. The ability to pivot—to change direction based on new information or shifting market conditions—is often the difference between success and failure. PayPal, for example, began as a cryptography company before shifting to a digital wallet model and finally becoming the payment platform we know today. This willingness to adapt allowed PayPal to survive and thrive in an industry littered with failed startups.

Adaptability is not just about responding to change; it is about anticipating it. The most successful entrepreneurs of the internet age were those who saw not just where the world was but where it was heading. They understood that the internet was not just a tool for communication but a platform for entirely new kinds of businesses. This foresight allowed them to position themselves as leaders in emerging markets.

Scaling with Precision

The internet has also taught us the importance of scalability. One of the defining features of digital businesses is their ability to grow quickly with relatively little additional cost. Companies like Google and Facebook built scalable models that allowed them to serve millions, then billions, of users without proportionally increasing their expenses.

However, scaling is not without its challenges. It requires careful planning and the right infrastructure. Many startups during the dot-com era failed because they attempted to scale too quickly, outpacing their resources and capabilities. Pets.com is a cautionary tale of a company that grew too fast, spending heavily on marketing and infrastructure without building a sustainable business model.

The lesson here is that growth must be strategic. Successful companies scale not just in size but in capability, ensuring that their systems, processes, and teams can handle increased demand. This requires a deep understanding of both the market and the operational requirements of the business.

The Role of Visionary Leadership

Behind every successful company is a visionary leader who dared to think differently. Jeff Bezos, Steve Jobs, Elon Musk, and others are often celebrated for their bold ideas and relentless pursuit of innovation. These leaders did more than create products—they inspired movements.

Visionary leadership is about more than just having a big idea; it is about the ability to rally others around that idea. Great leaders communicate a compelling vision that resonates with investors, employees, and customers alike. They also demonstrate resilience, pushing through challenges and setbacks to achieve their goals.

However, leadership is not without its pitfalls. The dot-com era is littered with examples of charismatic founders whose lack of discipline or focus led to their downfall. Vision without execution is a recipe for failure, and the best leaders balance bold thinking with meticulous planning.

Learning from Failures

The failures of the past are just as instructive as the successes. The dot-com bubble of the late 1990s and early 2000s serves as a stark reminder of the dangers of hype-driven markets. During this period, investors poured billions into internet startups, often with little regard for their business models or financial viability. When the bubble burst, many companies went under, wiping out trillions of dollars in market value.

Yet, from the ashes of the bubble emerged some of the most enduring companies of our time. Amazon, which saw its stock price plummet during the crash, emerged stronger by focusing on fundamentals—building a robust infrastructure, expanding its product offerings, and prioritizing customer satisfaction. Google, which was still in its infancy during the bubble, avoided the pitfalls of overvaluation and went on to become one of the most successful companies in history.

The lesson here is that failure is not the end; it is an opportunity to learn and grow. Entrepreneurs who are willing to analyze their mistakes and adapt their strategies are far more likely to succeed in the long run.

The Power of Collaboration

Another important lesson from the internet era is the power of collaboration. Many of the most successful innovations were the result of partnerships and ecosystems rather than individual efforts. Apple's App Store, for example, created a platform for thousands of developers to build and distribute their own software, fueling the success of the iPhone.

Collaboration extends beyond companies to include entire industries. The open-source movement, which began in the early days of the internet, has been a driving force behind technological innovation. By sharing knowledge and resources, developers have been able to build tools and platforms that benefit everyone.

For entrepreneurs, the takeaway is clear: success often requires working with others. Whether it is forming strategic partnerships, leveraging existing platforms, or contributing to open-source projects, collaboration can amplify your impact and accelerate your growth.

Looking Ahead

As we reflect on the lessons of the past, it is clear that we are entering a new phase of technological innovation. The challenges and opportunities of today are different from those of the internet era, but the principles remain the same. Timing, adaptability, scalability, leadership, resilience, and collaboration will continue to be the cornerstones of entrepreneurial success.

The internet taught us to think big—to imagine a world where borders disappear, information flows freely, and innovation knows no bounds. The next wave of technologies will push us to think even bigger, addressing problems that were once considered unsolvable and creating possibilities that were once unimaginable.

The lessons of the past are not just historical footnotes; they are guideposts for the future. By understanding what worked—and what didn't—we can navigate the complexities of the modern entrepreneurial landscape with confidence and clarity. As we move forward, let us carry these lessons with us, using them to build the future we want to see.

In this new age of entrepreneurship, the stakes are higher, the challenges greater, and the opportunities more profound. The question is not whether we can rise to the occasion but whether we will. The past has shown us what is possible; now it is up to us to create what comes next.

Chapter 2: The Convergence of Technologies

In today's rapidly evolving world, the pace of technological advancement is nothing short of breathtaking. Unlike the internet revolution, which was a singular event reshaping the global landscape, we now stand on the cusp of a transformation driven by the simultaneous rise of multiple groundbreaking technologies. Artificial intelligence (AI), biotechnology, quantum computing, renewable energy, blockchain, robotics, and space exploration are advancing at an unprecedented rate. Each of these domains alone has the potential to revolutionize industries, economies, and societies. But what is even more profound—and difficult to predict—is what happens when these technologies converge.

The Era of Convergence

Convergence refers to the point where two or more technologies intersect to create something greater than the sum of their parts. It is no longer sufficient to view these technologies in isolation. The future lies in their integration, where AI meets robotics to create autonomous machines, where blockchain underpins decentralized financial systems, or where quantum computing accelerates drug discovery through advancements in biotechnology.

Take, for example, the intersection of AI and healthcare. AI alone has transformed diagnostics, enabling doctors to detect diseases such as cancer with greater accuracy and speed than ever before. However, when AI is combined with advancements in biotechnology, it becomes possible to identify genetic markers for diseases and develop personalized treatments. Similarly, the convergence of renewable energy technologies with AI is optimizing energy grids, reducing waste, and creating smarter, more efficient cities.

This era of convergence is marked by complexity, interconnectedness, and opportunity. For entrepreneurs, it opens doors to innovations that were previously unimaginable. However, it also poses challenges: how do we predict and prepare for the unintended consequences of these powerful synergies?

The Key Technologies Driving Convergence

While many technologies are shaping the future, a few stand out as particularly influential in driving convergence:

1. Artificial Intelligence (AI)
AI is at the heart of technological convergence. Its ability to analyze massive datasets, recognize patterns, and make predictions is accelerating advancements across industries. AI is not just a tool; it is a foundational technology that amplifies the impact of others. For instance, in manufacturing, AI-powered robotics are creating smarter factories. In agriculture, AI algorithms are driving precision farming, reducing waste, and optimizing yields.

2. Blockchain
Blockchain's decentralized, transparent, and secure nature makes it a natural complement to many emerging technologies. In finance, blockchain is powering cryptocurrencies and decentralized finance (DeFi). In supply chain management, it is ensuring traceability and accountability. When combined with IoT, blockchain can secure data from billions of connected devices, opening new possibilities for smart cities and autonomous systems.

3. Biotechnology
Biotechnology has seen transformative advances in recent years, from CRISPR gene editing to synthetic biology. These innovations are reshaping medicine, agriculture, and even materials science. The convergence of biotech with AI has enabled faster drug discovery, while its integration with renewable energy is creating biofuels that could revolutionize energy consumption.

4. Quantum Computing
Quantum computing is poised to redefine what is computationally possible. Its ability to process massive datasets and solve problems exponentially faster than classical computers makes it a game-changer for industries like finance, logistics, and healthcare. Quantum computers can model molecular interactions at an unprecedented scale, accelerating the development of new drugs and materials.

5. Renewable Energy

The transition to renewable energy is one of the most critical challenges of our time. Solar, wind, and battery storage technologies are advancing rapidly, and their integration with AI and IoT is creating smarter, more efficient energy systems. For instance, AI-driven algorithms can predict energy demand and adjust grid operations in real time, reducing costs and emissions.

6. Robotics and Automation

Robotics is no longer confined to factory floors. Today, robots are performing surgery, delivering goods, and exploring other planets. When combined with AI, these machines become more autonomous, adaptive, and capable of performing complex tasks. The convergence of robotics with other technologies like blockchain and IoT is also enabling new possibilities, such as secure supply chain automation.

7. Space Exploration

The final frontier is becoming more accessible thanks to advancements in reusable rockets, satellite technology, and robotics. Space exploration is converging with AI and telecommunications, enabling the development of satellite networks that can provide global internet access and monitor climate change in real time.

Real-World Examples of Convergence

The power of convergence is not theoretical—it is already transforming industries and creating new opportunities:

Healthcare:

The integration of AI, biotechnology, and wearable technology is driving the era of personalized medicine. Companies like 23andMe are using genetic data to provide insights into health risks, while AI-powered platforms analyze this data to recommend preventative measures. Furthermore, robotic surgery systems like Intuitive Surgical's da Vinci are combining robotics with AI to enhance precision and reduce recovery times.

Finance:

Blockchain and AI are reshaping the financial landscape.

Decentralized finance platforms like Aave and Uniswap are using blockchain to democratize access to financial services. At the same time, AI-driven algorithms are improving fraud detection, credit scoring, and investment strategies.

Energy:
Renewable energy technologies are converging with AI and IoT to create smart grids that optimize energy consumption and reduce waste. Companies like Tesla are integrating solar panels, battery storage, and electric vehicles into seamless systems that support sustainable living.

Agriculture:
Precision farming is a prime example of technological convergence in agriculture. AI analyzes data from IoT sensors placed in fields to optimize irrigation, fertilization, and pest control. Drones equipped with AI and imaging technologies monitor crop health and yield predictions.

Transportation:
The rise of autonomous vehicles is perhaps the most visible example of convergence in action. Companies like Tesla and Waymo are combining AI, IoT, and renewable energy technologies to create self-driving, electric cars that are safer and more efficient than traditional vehicles.

The Opportunities for Entrepreneurs

For entrepreneurs, convergence presents a unique opportunity to create transformative innovations. By identifying intersections between technologies, they can address complex problems and unlock new markets. For instance, a startup could combine AI and blockchain to improve supply chain transparency or use quantum computing and biotechnology to accelerate vaccine development.

However, seizing these opportunities requires a mindset shift. Entrepreneurs must think holistically, understanding how different technologies interact and amplify each other. They must also build diverse teams with expertise across multiple domains, as the challenges of convergence often require interdisciplinary solutions.

Challenges of Convergence

While the potential of convergence is immense, it is not without challenges:

1. Complexity:
As technologies converge, systems become more complex, making them harder to design, implement, and regulate. Entrepreneurs must navigate this complexity while ensuring their solutions remain user-friendly and scalable.

2. Ethical Concerns:
The convergence of technologies often raises ethical questions. For example, combining AI with biotechnology could lead to advancements in gene editing, but it also poses risks of misuse or unintended consequences. Entrepreneurs must address these concerns proactively, embedding ethics into their innovations.

3. Regulation:
The rapid pace of technological change often outstrips regulatory frameworks. Entrepreneurs working at the intersection of technologies must navigate uncertain legal landscapes and advocate for policies that support innovation while protecting public interests.

4. Resource Intensity:
Developing and deploying convergent technologies often requires significant resources, from funding to talent. Entrepreneurs must find ways to access these resources while maintaining agility.

The Future of Convergence

As we look to the future, the possibilities of convergence are both exciting and daunting. The next decade will likely see the emergence of industries and companies that we cannot yet imagine. However, history has shown us that with great technological progress comes great responsibility.

Entrepreneurs have a critical role to play in shaping this future. By embracing convergence, they can create solutions that address humanity's most pressing challenges, from climate change to global health crises. But they must also approach this work with humility, recognizing the potential risks and unintended consequences of their innovations.

The era of convergence is not just about technology; it is about people. It is about using our collective knowledge and creativity to build a better world. For those willing to rise to the challenge, the opportunities are endless—and the time to act is now.

In this new age of entrepreneurship, convergence is the ultimate frontier. It is where innovation happens, where problems are solved, and where the future is built. Let us embrace it, with all its complexity and potential, as we work to create a world that is smarter, healthier, and more sustainable than ever before.

Chapter 3: The Bold New Era of Innovation

The world is on the cusp of a profound transformation, fueled by the simultaneous rise of multiple groundbreaking technologies and an increasingly interconnected global economy. This new era of innovation is characterized by opportunities that were once the realm of science fiction but are now becoming realities. Entrepreneurs today find themselves in an unprecedented position: with tools, knowledge, and resources at their fingertips, they can dream bigger and act faster than at any other time in history.

However, this bold new era is not without its challenges. The pace of change is accelerating, global competition is fierce, and the problems we face as a planet—climate change, inequality, resource scarcity, and public health crises—are more complex and interconnected than ever. Yet, it is precisely in these challenges that the greatest opportunities lie. This chapter explores why now is the most exciting time to be an entrepreneur, the tools and resources that make this moment unique, and the mindset required to thrive in this bold new era of innovation.

The Unique Opportunities of Today

The opportunities of today are unparalleled. Technological advancements have created entirely new fields of exploration, from AI and quantum computing to renewable energy and space technology. Each of these domains is ripe with potential for entrepreneurs who are willing to take risks and push boundaries.

1. **The Intersection of Technology and Humanity:**
   Innovations today are not just changing industries; they are reshaping how we live and interact. For example, AI is enhancing accessibility for individuals with disabilities, while biotechnology is enabling personalized medicine tailored to a person's genetic makeup. Entrepreneurs who focus on solving human-centric problems can create meaningful, lasting impact.

2. **Global Markets, Local Solutions:**
   The internet and digital tools have made it possible to build businesses that are global from day one. However, the best innovations often arise from addressing local problems. Entrepreneurs who identify solutions that work in specific communities or regions can scale those solutions to larger markets. For instance, renewable energy startups in Africa are creating solar power solutions that could be applied globally.

3. **Decentralized Innovation:**
   Unlike previous eras where innovation was concentrated in hubs like Silicon Valley, today's innovation ecosystem is distributed. Talent and resources are no longer limited by geography. With remote work, digital collaboration tools, and crowdfunding platforms, entrepreneurs from any corner of the world can build transformative companies.

4. **Big, Bad Problems:**
   The most significant challenges facing humanity—climate change, food security, healthcare access—also present the greatest opportunities for innovation. Entrepreneurs willing to tackle these issues head-on have the potential to not only build successful businesses but also create a better world.

The Tools of the Trade

One of the defining features of this era is the abundance of tools and resources available to entrepreneurs. What was once the domain of large corporations or government-funded institutions is now accessible to individuals and small teams.

1. **Cloud Computing and AI:**
   Cloud computing has democratized access to powerful computing resources, allowing startups to build and scale applications without investing in expensive infrastructure. Combined with AI, entrepreneurs can analyze data, automate processes, and develop innovative products more efficiently than ever.

2. **Open Source and Low-Code Platforms:**
   Open-source software and low-code platforms have lowered the barriers to entry for building technology. Entrepreneurs can now prototype and deploy solutions quickly, focusing on innovation rather than technical complexities.

3. **Global Connectivity:**
   The ubiquity of the internet and advancements in telecommunications mean that entrepreneurs can reach audiences and collaborators around the globe. Tools like Zoom, Slack, and GitHub enable seamless remote collaboration, while social media platforms provide a direct line to customers and stakeholders.

4. **Access to Capital:**
   Crowdfunding platforms like Kickstarter, peer-to-peer lending networks, and venture capital firms have made it easier than ever to secure funding. Additionally, decentralized finance (DeFi) is opening up new avenues for raising capital, particularly in underserved markets.

5. **Education and Skill Development:**
   Online learning platforms like Coursera, edX, and Udemy have democratized access to high-quality education. Entrepreneurs can learn new skills, from coding to marketing, at their own pace, empowering them to build

better businesses.

The Bold Entrepreneurial Mindset

While tools and resources are important, the defining factor of success in this new era is mindset. The challenges of today require entrepreneurs to think differently, act boldly, and adapt constantly.

1. **Think Big, Start Small:**
   Bold entrepreneurs think on a grand scale, envisioning how their innovations can reshape industries or solve pressing global challenges. However, they also understand the importance of starting small—testing their ideas, learning from feedback, and iterating rapidly. For example, Elon Musk's vision of a multi-planetary species started with small-scale rocket prototypes before SpaceX achieved its groundbreaking successes.

2. **Resilience in the Face of Failure:**
   The path to innovation is rarely linear. Entrepreneurs must embrace failure as an integral part of the journey. Each setback is an opportunity to learn, pivot, and improve. Companies like Airbnb and Slack faced early struggles but succeeded by adapting and refining their models.

3. **Collaboration over Competition:**
   In a world where resources and talent are abundant, collaboration often outweighs competition. Entrepreneurs who build partnerships, leverage ecosystems, and share knowledge are better positioned to succeed. The rise of open innovation models, where companies collaborate on solving shared challenges, reflects this mindset.

4. **Ethics and Responsibility:**
   Boldness in innovation must be tempered with responsibility. Entrepreneurs today have a duty to consider the ethical implications of their work. Whether it is

addressing biases in AI algorithms or ensuring sustainability in production processes, responsible innovation builds trust and creates lasting value.

5. **Adaptability and Agility:**
   The rapid pace of change means that entrepreneurs must remain flexible. Business models that work today may be obsolete tomorrow. Successful entrepreneurs stay ahead by anticipating trends, experimenting with new approaches, and continuously learning.

Case Studies of Bold Innovation

1. **Beyond Meat:**
   The plant-based meat company exemplifies bold thinking in addressing a global issue—sustainable food production. By leveraging advances in food science and biotechnology, Beyond Meat created products that mimic the taste and texture of meat, appealing to both vegetarians and meat-eaters. Their success highlights the potential of combining innovation with purpose.

2. **SpaceX:**
   SpaceX's audacious goal of making space exploration accessible and affordable has revolutionized the aerospace industry. Through innovations like reusable rockets, the company has not only reduced costs but also paved the way for future missions to Mars.

3. **Tesla:**
   Tesla's focus on electric vehicles, renewable energy, and battery technology demonstrates the power of convergence. The company has disrupted the automotive industry while advancing the transition to sustainable energy.

4. **Stripe:**
   Stripe's mission to simplify online payments has empowered millions of businesses worldwide. By focusing

on developer-friendly solutions and expanding into global markets, Stripe has become a cornerstone of the digital economy.

Navigating the Challenges of Bold Innovation

While the opportunities are immense, the path of bold innovation is not without obstacles. Entrepreneurs must be prepared to navigate a range of challenges:

1. **Managing Risk:**
   Bold ventures often involve significant risks, from financial investments to reputational stakes. Entrepreneurs must develop strategies to mitigate these risks, balancing ambition with caution.

2. **Navigating Regulation:**
   As technologies like AI and blockchain evolve, regulatory frameworks often lag behind. Entrepreneurs must stay informed about legal developments and work proactively with regulators to ensure compliance.

3. **Balancing Growth and Sustainability:**
   Rapid growth can strain resources and lead to burnout. Entrepreneurs must focus on sustainable practices, ensuring that their businesses are built to last.

4. **Overcoming Skepticism:**
   Bold ideas often face skepticism or resistance, particularly when they challenge established norms. Entrepreneurs must be skilled communicators, articulating their vision and building trust with stakeholders.

The Future of Bold Innovation

The bold new era of innovation is just beginning. As technologies continue to advance and global challenges become more pressing, the need for courageous, creative entrepreneurs will only grow. The future belongs to those who are willing to take risks, embrace uncertainty, and push the boundaries of what is possible.

This era is not just about building businesses; it is about shaping the world. Entrepreneurs have the power to create solutions that improve lives, protect the planet, and unlock human potential. By embracing boldness and purpose, they can drive progress and leave a legacy that transcends profit.

The opportunities are endless, but the time to act is now. In this bold new era of innovation, the world is waiting for those who dare to dream—and to build.

Chapter 4: The Global Entrepreneur

The rise of the internet and digital tools has shattered the geographical barriers that once confined innovation and opportunity to a select few regions of the world. We are now living in an era where entrepreneurship is no longer bound by physical borders, where talent, ideas, and resources can emerge from anywhere and impact everywhere. The "global entrepreneur" is not just a concept—it is a necessity in a world that is increasingly interconnected and interdependent.

This chapter explores the rise of global entrepreneurship, the tools and trends driving this phenomenon, the opportunities it presents, and the challenges entrepreneurs must navigate to succeed in this borderless world. It is a call to action for entrepreneurs to embrace a global mindset, recognizing that innovation knows no boundaries and that the future of business lies in collaboration across continents.

The Rise of Global Entrepreneurship

For much of modern history, entrepreneurship was a local affair. Businesses catered to the needs of their immediate communities, and even large companies often had regional focuses. The industrial revolution began to change this, but it was the rise of the internet that truly democratized access to markets and resources.

Today, an entrepreneur in Nairobi can design a product for customers in New York, while a startup in Bangalore can collaborate with developers in Berlin. This global connectivity has created an environment where the barriers to entry have been lowered, enabling innovators from all corners of the world to participate in and contribute to the global economy.

The rise of global entrepreneurship has been driven by several key trends:

1. **Access to Digital Tools:**
    Platforms like Shopify, Zoom, and Slack have made it easier than ever to build, run, and scale a business from anywhere. Entrepreneurs can now access global markets, hire remote teams, and manage operations with minimal infrastructure.

2. **Global Capital Flow:**
    Venture capital, once concentrated in Silicon Valley, is now increasingly global. Investors are recognizing the potential of startups in emerging markets and are channeling resources to entrepreneurs in Africa, Southeast Asia, Latin America, and beyond. Crowdfunding and decentralized finance have further democratized access to funding.

3. **Rise of E-Commerce:**
    The explosion of e-commerce has opened global markets to small businesses and individual entrepreneurs. Platforms like Amazon, Etsy, and Alibaba allow sellers to reach customers worldwide without the need for traditional distribution networks.

4. **Remote Work Revolution:**
    The COVID-19 pandemic accelerated the adoption of remote work, proving that businesses can operate

effectively without being tied to a single location. This has enabled companies to tap into talent from across the globe, creating truly international teams.

5. **Cross-Cultural Collaboration:**
   As cultural and linguistic barriers continue to erode, thanks to tools like Google Translate and platforms like LinkedIn, collaboration across borders has become more seamless. Entrepreneurs can now work with diverse teams, combining perspectives to create innovative solutions.

Opportunities for Global Entrepreneurs

The global landscape offers unique opportunities for entrepreneurs willing to embrace a borderless mindset.

1. **Access to Diverse Talent Pools:**
   The days when innovation was confined to Silicon Valley are over. Talented developers, designers, and business professionals can be found in every corner of the world. By building diverse teams, entrepreneurs can harness a wide range of skills, perspectives, and experiences to create products that resonate globally.

2. **Solving Universal Problems:**
   Many of the challenges we face today—climate change, access to healthcare, education inequality—are global in nature. Entrepreneurs who tackle these issues can create solutions with worldwide impact. For example, startups working on renewable energy or digital healthcare platforms have the potential to scale rapidly across borders.

3. **Tapping into Emerging Markets:**
   Emerging markets represent some of the fastest-growing economies in the world. Countries like India, Brazil, and Nigeria are experiencing a surge in internet adoption, middle-class growth, and entrepreneurial activity. These markets offer untapped opportunities for businesses that

can meet their unique needs.

4. **Leveraging Global Platforms:**
   Platforms like Upwork, Amazon Web Services, and Stripe enable entrepreneurs to build, fund, and scale their ventures with ease. These tools provide access to customers, infrastructure, and financial systems that were once out of reach for small businesses.

5. **Cultural Innovation:**
   Entrepreneurs operating in a global context can draw inspiration from diverse cultures, creating products and services that blend the best of multiple traditions. This cultural cross-pollination often leads to innovative solutions that appeal to a broad audience.

Challenges of Global Entrepreneurship

While the opportunities are immense, operating on a global scale also comes with its own set of challenges. Entrepreneurs must be prepared to navigate a complex and dynamic landscape.

1. **Navigating Regulatory Environments:**
   Each country has its own regulations regarding business operations, taxation, data privacy, and employment laws. Entrepreneurs must navigate these diverse legal frameworks to ensure compliance, which can be both time-consuming and costly.

2. **Cultural Sensitivity:**
   Operating in a global market requires an understanding of cultural differences. Products or marketing strategies that resonate in one region may not work in another. Entrepreneurs must invest time in researching and understanding the preferences, values, and customs of their target markets.

3. **Logistical Complexity:**
   Managing supply chains, shipping, and distribution across borders can be challenging, particularly in regions with underdeveloped infrastructure. Entrepreneurs must find reliable partners and build resilient logistics networks.

4. **Currency and Payment Challenges:**
   Dealing with multiple currencies and payment systems can create friction for global businesses. While platforms like Stripe and PayPal have simplified cross-border transactions, entrepreneurs must still account for exchange rates, transaction fees, and local banking regulations.

5. **Competition:**
   A global market means global competition. Entrepreneurs must differentiate themselves not only from local competitors but also from established international players. Building a strong brand and delivering exceptional value are critical to standing out.

Strategies for Success as a Global Entrepreneur

To thrive in the global landscape, entrepreneurs must adopt specific strategies that enable them to navigate challenges and seize opportunities.

1. **Adopt a Global Mindset:**
   Successful global entrepreneurs view the world as their marketplace. They think beyond borders and design their products, services, and strategies to appeal to diverse audiences.

2. **Leverage Technology:**
   Digital tools are the backbone of global entrepreneurship. From e-commerce platforms to remote collaboration software, entrepreneurs must embrace technology to streamline operations and expand their reach.

3. **Build Cross-Cultural Teams:**
   Diverse teams bring diverse perspectives, which can lead to more innovative solutions. Entrepreneurs should seek out team members from different cultural backgrounds and foster an inclusive environment that encourages collaboration.

4. **Focus on Localization:**
   While thinking globally is important, acting locally is equally critical. Entrepreneurs must adapt their products and services to meet the specific needs of different markets, whether it's customizing language, pricing, or user experiences.

5. **Partner Strategically:**
   Building strong partnerships is essential for navigating the complexities of global business. Entrepreneurs should seek out local partners who understand the market dynamics and can provide valuable insights and support.

6. **Stay Agile:**
   The global business environment is constantly changing. Entrepreneurs must remain flexible, ready to adapt to new regulations, market trends, and customer preferences. Agility is key to surviving and thriving in a competitive landscape.

Case Studies of Global Entrepreneurs

1. **Shopify:**
   Founded in Canada, Shopify has become a global platform for e-commerce, empowering entrepreneurs worldwide to build and scale online stores. By providing tools that work seamlessly across borders, Shopify has enabled businesses of all sizes to tap into global markets.

2. **Paystack:**
   Based in Nigeria, Paystack revolutionized online payments

in Africa by creating a seamless and secure payment platform tailored to local needs. After its acquisition by Stripe, Paystack is now scaling its solutions to other regions, demonstrating the power of starting local and thinking global.

3. **ByteDance:**
    The parent company of TikTok, ByteDance exemplifies the potential of global entrepreneurship. By combining cutting-edge AI with culturally relevant content strategies, ByteDance has created a platform that resonates with users worldwide.

4. **Grab:**
    Founded in Southeast Asia, Grab started as a ride-hailing app and expanded into food delivery, digital payments, and financial services. Its success lies in its deep understanding of local markets combined with a global vision for growth.

The Future of Global Entrepreneurship

The future of entrepreneurship is undoubtedly global. As technology continues to break down barriers and connect people across continents, the opportunities for global innovation will only expand. Entrepreneurs who embrace this borderless mindset will be at the forefront of creating solutions that address humanity's greatest challenges and unlock unprecedented potential.

The rise of the global entrepreneur is not just about business—it is about building a world where innovation is inclusive, equitable, and transformative. The next wave of great companies will not come from one city or country; they will come from everywhere.

In this bold new era, the question is not whether you can participate in the global economy but how. The tools, resources, and opportunities are there. It's time to think big, act boldly, and embrace the limitless possibilities of global entrepreneurship.

Chapter 5: Tackling Big, Bad Problems

Throughout history, humanity has faced challenges that seemed insurmountable at the time: eradicating diseases, connecting distant lands, and even venturing into outer space. Each of these feats required bold thinking, innovative approaches, and a willingness to confront problems that others deemed impossible. In today's world, we are presented with a new set of "big, bad problems"—climate change, global health crises, food security, and systemic inequality, to name a few. These challenges are daunting in their scope, complexity, and urgency, but they also represent extraordinary opportunities for innovation.

Entrepreneurs willing to tackle these issues head-on are not only positioned to create transformative businesses but also to leave a lasting impact on the world. This chapter explores why big, bad problems demand bold solutions, the frameworks for addressing them, and the mindset required to succeed in this critical endeavor.

The Nature of Big, Bad Problems

Big, bad problems share several defining characteristics that make them both challenging and compelling for entrepreneurs.

1. **Complexity:**
   These problems are often deeply interconnected, involving multiple systems and stakeholders. For example, addressing climate change requires tackling emissions from energy, transportation, agriculture, and manufacturing while navigating political, economic, and social dynamics.

2. **Scale:**
   Big, bad problems affect millions—if not billions—of people. They are not confined to a single country or community but are global in nature. For instance, the COVID-19 pandemic underscored how a health crisis in one region can ripple across the world.

3. **Urgency:**
   These challenges demand immediate attention. Delaying action can exacerbate the problem, leading to irreversible damage. For example, inaction on climate change could lead to catastrophic environmental and economic consequences.

4. **Resource Intensity:**
   Solving these problems often requires significant investment in time, money, and talent. Entrepreneurs must be prepared to navigate resource constraints while scaling their solutions effectively.

Why Big, Bad Problems Are Worth Tackling

While daunting, big, bad problems are uniquely rewarding for entrepreneurs who are willing to take them on.

1. **Meaningful Impact:**
   Entrepreneurs who address these challenges have the opportunity to improve lives on a massive scale. For instance, renewable energy companies are not just profitable—they are helping to transition the world toward sustainability.

2. **Market Opportunities:**
   Big problems often represent untapped markets. Consumers, governments, and organizations are increasingly seeking solutions to pressing issues, creating demand for innovative products and services.

3. **Competitive Advantage:**
   Entrepreneurs who solve complex problems gain a significant competitive edge. Their solutions are harder to replicate, creating barriers to entry for competitors.

4. **Attracting Talent and Capital:**
   Purpose-driven companies often attract top talent and investors who are aligned with their mission. Employees and stakeholders are increasingly motivated by the potential to contribute to meaningful change.

Frameworks for Tackling Big, Bad Problems

Successfully addressing these challenges requires more than ambition—it demands a systematic approach. Entrepreneurs can benefit from frameworks that help them break down complexity, identify opportunities, and execute solutions effectively.

1. **Define the Problem Clearly:**
   The first step in solving a big problem is understanding it. Entrepreneurs must identify the root causes, stakeholders, and systems involved. This often involves extensive research, data collection, and stakeholder engagement.

   Example: In addressing food insecurity, entrepreneurs

must analyze factors such as agricultural inefficiency, supply chain gaps, and affordability issues.

2. **Focus on Scalable Solutions:**
   Solutions to big problems must be scalable to achieve meaningful impact. Entrepreneurs should design products and services that can grow rapidly without requiring proportional increases in resources.

   Example: Solar panel companies like SunPower focus on modular, scalable technologies that can be deployed in diverse settings.

3. **Leverage Technology:**
   Technology is often the key to unlocking innovative solutions. AI, blockchain, biotechnology, and IoT can help entrepreneurs address challenges in ways that were previously impossible.

   Example: AI-driven platforms like BlueDot use data analytics to predict and track disease outbreaks, enabling faster responses to global health crises.

4. **Collaborate Across Sectors:**
   Big problems require collective action. Entrepreneurs must build partnerships with governments, NGOs, and other businesses to amplify their impact. Collaboration can provide access to resources, expertise, and networks.

   Example: Gavi, the Vaccine Alliance, brings together public and private partners to improve global immunization access.

5. **Measure Impact:**
   Success in tackling big problems goes beyond profit—it requires measurable social and environmental impact. Entrepreneurs should establish clear metrics and track progress over time.

   Example: Social enterprises like TOMS Shoes track the

number of shoes donated and communities served as part of their impact reporting.

The Mindset for Tackling Big, Bad Problems

Addressing massive challenges requires a specific mindset. Entrepreneurs must cultivate resilience, adaptability, and vision to navigate the complexities of these problems.

1. **Think Long-Term:**
   Big problems cannot be solved overnight. Entrepreneurs must adopt a long-term perspective, balancing immediate wins with sustained efforts.

   Example: Tesla's journey to revolutionize the automotive industry required years of research, development, and market education before electric vehicles gained mainstream acceptance.

2. **Embrace Failure as a Learning Tool:**
   Tackling complex problems often involves trial and error. Entrepreneurs must view failures as opportunities to learn, iterate, and improve.

   Example: SpaceX experienced multiple rocket failures before achieving its first successful launch, ultimately redefining space exploration.

3. **Stay Mission-Driven:**
   Purpose is a powerful motivator. Entrepreneurs who are deeply committed to their mission are better equipped to weather challenges and inspire their teams.

   Example: Patagonia's unwavering commitment to sustainability has earned it loyal customers and a reputation for ethical leadership.

4. **Foster Collaboration and Inclusivity:**
   Solving big problems requires diverse perspectives. Entrepreneurs must build teams and partnerships that reflect the complexity of the challenges they are addressing.

   Example: The team behind the Human Genome Project included scientists, researchers, and organizations from around the world, enabling breakthroughs in genetics.

5. **Adapt to Change:**
   The landscape of big problems is constantly evolving. Entrepreneurs must remain flexible, ready to pivot as new information and opportunities emerge.

   Example: During the COVID-19 pandemic, many companies shifted their operations to produce essential supplies like masks and ventilators.

Case Studies of Entrepreneurs Tackling Big, Bad Problems

1. **Beyond Meat:**
   The company addresses the environmental impact of traditional meat production by creating plant-based alternatives. By combining food science and sustainability, Beyond Meat is tackling climate change and food security simultaneously.

2. **Zipline:**
   This drone delivery company is revolutionizing healthcare logistics by delivering medical supplies to remote areas. Zipline's innovative approach is saving lives in regions with limited infrastructure.

3. **CureVac:**
   A biotechnology company focused on mRNA-based therapies and vaccines, CureVac is addressing global health challenges, including the COVID-19 pandemic.

4. **Oatly:**
   By creating plant-based dairy alternatives, Oatly is reducing the environmental impact of traditional dairy production while meeting growing consumer demand for sustainable products.

5. **Gravity Water:**
   This social enterprise provides communities with clean drinking water by combining rainwater harvesting and filtration technology.

Overcoming Barriers to Tackling Big Problems

Despite the opportunities, entrepreneurs face significant barriers when addressing large-scale challenges. Overcoming these barriers requires creative problem-solving and strategic action.

1. **Resource Constraints:**
   Entrepreneurs often lack the resources needed to tackle big problems. Building strong networks, securing funding, and leveraging partnerships can help bridge this gap.

2. **Resistance to Change:**
   Disrupting established systems often meets resistance from incumbents. Entrepreneurs must build trust, educate stakeholders, and demonstrate the value of their solutions.

3. **Complexity of Stakeholders:**
   Big problems often involve multiple stakeholders with competing interests. Entrepreneurs must navigate these dynamics skillfully, building consensus and finding common ground.

The Future of Tackling Big, Bad Problems

As technology continues to advance and global awareness of pressing challenges grows, the opportunities for entrepreneurs to address big problems will only expand. The next generation of innovators will play a pivotal role in shaping a more sustainable, equitable, and resilient world.

Tackling big, bad problems is not just about creating businesses—it is about driving systemic change. Entrepreneurs who rise to the occasion will not only build successful companies but also leave a legacy that transcends profit. The path is challenging, but the rewards—both personal and societal—are immense.

The world needs bold thinkers and doers who are willing to confront the challenges of our time. The question is not whether these problems can be solved, but who will step up to solve them. The opportunities are there, the tools are available, and the time to act is now.

Chapter 6: Designing the Modern Tech Incubator

In an era defined by rapid technological progress and global connectivity, the role of a tech incubator has evolved dramatically. What once worked for early pioneers like Y Combinator or TechStars—geographically focused, localized hubs of innovation—is no longer sufficient in today's world. Entrepreneurs are no longer bound by physical locations, and technology itself demands a new approach to nurturing startups. A modern tech incubator must be a dynamic, inclusive, and global platform that equips entrepreneurs to tackle complex challenges and seize emerging opportunities.

This chapter explores the fundamental principles, structures, and strategies required to design a tech incubator for the modern era. It highlights the challenges and opportunities inherent in this process and offers a roadmap for building an ecosystem that empowers entrepreneurs to thrive in a borderless, fast-paced world.

The Evolving Role of Tech Incubators

Tech incubators have always served as catalysts for innovation. They provide entrepreneurs with critical resources—mentorship, funding, infrastructure, and networks—to turn ideas into viable businesses. However, the nature of entrepreneurship has changed in several ways:

1. **Globalization of Innovation:**
   Talent, resources, and opportunities are no longer concentrated in a few geographic hubs like Silicon Valley. Innovation is now a global phenomenon, with entrepreneurs emerging from diverse regions and backgrounds.

2. **Convergence of Technologies:**
   Modern startups often operate at the intersection of multiple technologies, such as AI, blockchain, and biotechnology. Incubators must adapt to this complexity by offering specialized expertise and resources.

3. **Accelerated Pace of Innovation:**
   Startups today face intense pressure to move quickly, iterate rapidly, and scale efficiently. Incubators must foster agility while providing stability and support.

4. **Focus on Purpose-Driven Innovation:**
   Entrepreneurs are increasingly motivated by a desire to address societal challenges, such as climate change, healthcare access, and economic inequality. Incubators must align with these values to attract and support mission-driven founders.

Core Principles of the Modern Tech Incubator

To succeed in this new landscape, a tech incubator must be built on the following principles:

1. **Global Accessibility:**
   A modern incubator must operate without borders, providing access to resources and networks regardless of an entrepreneur's location. Digital platforms and remote collaboration tools are essential to creating an inclusive ecosystem.

2. **Diversity and Inclusion:**
   The best solutions arise from diverse perspectives. Incubators should actively seek out entrepreneurs from underrepresented communities, fostering an environment where diverse ideas and approaches can thrive.

3. **Focus on Scalability:**
   Startups must be designed to grow. Incubators should prioritize scalable business models and provide resources that help founders reach global markets.

4. **Interdisciplinary Collaboration:**
   With technology increasingly converging across domains, incubators must facilitate cross-disciplinary learning and collaboration, enabling entrepreneurs to leverage multiple fields of expertise.

5. **Sustainability and Impact:**
   Beyond profit, incubators must encourage startups to create solutions that are environmentally, socially, and economically sustainable.

Key Components of a Modern Tech Incubator

Designing a successful tech incubator involves integrating several key components:

1. **Digital Infrastructure:**
   A modern incubator must invest in robust digital infrastructure to support virtual engagement, mentorship, and resource sharing. Platforms for video conferencing,

project management, and knowledge sharing are critical.

2. **Global Networks:**
   Entrepreneurs need access to a global network of mentors, investors, and industry experts. Incubators should cultivate relationships across regions and industries, creating opportunities for startups to connect with stakeholders worldwide.

3. **Sector-Specific Expertise:**
   Given the complexity of modern technologies, incubators must offer specialized support in areas like AI, robotics, biotech, and renewable energy. This includes access to domain experts, research facilities, and technical training.

4. **Funding and Capital Access:**
   A core function of any incubator is helping startups secure funding. This includes connecting entrepreneurs with venture capitalists, angel investors, and crowdfunding platforms, as well as providing seed funding directly.

5. **Mentorship and Coaching:**
   Entrepreneurs need guidance from experienced mentors who can help them navigate challenges, refine their strategies, and build strong teams. Mentorship programs should be tailored to the specific needs of each startup.

6. **Community and Peer Learning:**
   Building a sense of community is essential for fostering collaboration and resilience. Entrepreneurs should have opportunities to learn from and support one another through networking events, workshops, and collaborative projects.

Strategies for Designing a Modern Tech Incubator

Building an effective incubator requires strategic planning and execution. The following steps can help incubator founders create a thriving ecosystem:

1. **Identify a Clear Mission:**
   A successful incubator starts with a clear mission and focus. Whether it's supporting startups in a specific industry, fostering innovation in underserved regions, or addressing global challenges, the mission should guide all decisions.

   Example: Greentown Labs, a climate-tech incubator, focuses exclusively on startups developing solutions to combat climate change.

2. **Leverage Technology:**
   Digital tools can expand the reach and impact of an incubator. Virtual programs, online mentorship, and global hackathons enable participation from entrepreneurs who might otherwise be excluded.

   Example: Startup School by Y Combinator offers free, online resources to entrepreneurs worldwide, democratizing access to mentorship and expertise.

3. **Create Hybrid Models:**
   While digital platforms are essential, in-person collaboration remains valuable. A hybrid model that combines physical hubs with virtual programming can offer the best of both worlds.

   Example: Station F in Paris combines a physical campus with digital resources to support startups from around the globe.

4. **Build Partnerships:**
   Collaboration with universities, corporations, and government agencies can provide startups with access to research, funding, and market opportunities. These partnerships can also help incubators scale their impact.

   Example: The MIT Startup Exchange connects startups with corporate partners to accelerate innovation.

5. **Focus on Measurable Outcomes:**
   Incubators should define success metrics—such as the number of startups launched, jobs created, or funding secured—and track their progress over time. Impact measurement ensures accountability and helps attract stakeholders.

   Example: 500 Startups publishes annual reports detailing its portfolio's performance and social impact.

Challenges in Designing Modern Tech Incubators

While the potential of modern incubators is immense, they also face significant challenges:

1. **Resource Allocation:**
   Supporting startups across diverse regions and industries requires substantial resources. Incubators must prioritize efficiently and secure sustainable funding models.

2. **Balancing Inclusivity and Focus:**
   While inclusivity is essential, incubators must also maintain focus to deliver targeted support. Striking the right balance can be challenging.

3. **Navigating Global Regulations:**
   Operating in a global context means dealing with diverse legal and regulatory frameworks. Incubators must provide startups with the knowledge and resources to navigate these complexities.

4. **Adapting to Rapid Change:**
   The pace of technological change means that incubators must constantly evolve their programs and offerings. Staying ahead of trends is critical to remaining relevant.

Case Studies of Modern Tech Incubators

1. **Y Combinator:**
   While rooted in Silicon Valley, Y Combinator has adapted to the global landscape by offering remote programs and expanding its reach. Its online Startup School exemplifies the potential of digital-first incubators.

2. **Greentown Labs:**
   This climate-tech incubator focuses exclusively on sustainability startups, providing specialized resources like prototyping labs and connections to energy companies.

3. **MassChallenge:**
   With locations across the globe, MassChallenge supports startups in diverse industries and markets. Its zero-equity model ensures accessibility for entrepreneurs at all stages.

4. **Station F:**
   As the world's largest startup campus, Station F combines physical infrastructure with a vibrant online community. Its focus on inclusivity has attracted startups from over 60 countries.

5. **Plug and Play:**
   This global innovation platform connects startups with corporations, fostering collaboration and creating opportunities for scaling solutions across industries.

The Future of Tech Incubators

As entrepreneurship continues to evolve, the role of tech incubators will become even more critical. The incubators of the future will need to:

1. **Integrate Emerging Technologies:**
   From AI-driven mentorship platforms to blockchain-based funding mechanisms, technology will play an increasingly

central role in incubator operations.

2. **Foster Global Collaboration:**
   Incubators must act as bridges between regions, industries, and cultures, enabling startups to tackle global challenges collectively.

3. **Champion Purpose-Driven Innovation:**
   Addressing societal challenges will be at the heart of future incubators. Programs will prioritize startups that create solutions with measurable social and environmental impact.

4. **Adapt to New Business Models:**
   As entrepreneurship evolves, incubators will experiment with new funding structures, such as revenue-sharing models or decentralized investment platforms.

Conclusion

The modern tech incubator is more than a space—it is a global, dynamic ecosystem that empowers entrepreneurs to build the future. By embracing inclusivity, leveraging technology, and fostering collaboration, incubators can become engines of innovation that address the most pressing challenges of our time.

The next generation of entrepreneurs is ready to rise to the occasion. They need incubators designed for a borderless, fast-paced world—incubators that provide not just resources but also inspiration, guidance, and community. For those willing to lead the charge, the opportunities to shape the future are limitless.

Chapter 7: From Vision to Reality

Every great innovation begins as a spark of inspiration—a vision for something new, transformative, and impactful. But turning that vision into reality is a complex, demanding process. It requires more than just a good idea; it takes strategic planning, resilient execution, and a relentless drive to overcome obstacles. For entrepreneurs, the journey from vision to reality is the ultimate test of their creativity, adaptability, and perseverance.

This chapter explores the critical steps involved in transforming a bold vision into a tangible and successful reality. From building strong teams to navigating challenges and scaling operations, it provides a roadmap for entrepreneurs to bridge the gap between ideas and implementation.

The Foundation: Defining a Clear Vision

The journey from vision to reality begins with clarity. A compelling vision acts as a guiding star, providing direction and inspiration for both the entrepreneur and their team.

1. **What Makes a Great Vision?**
   A powerful vision is both ambitious and grounded in reality. It articulates a bold goal while remaining achievable through strategic effort. For example, Elon Musk's vision of a multi-planetary species is audacious, yet SpaceX's step-by-step approach makes it tangible.

2. **Aligning Vision with Purpose:**
   Entrepreneurs must ensure their vision aligns with a clear purpose—something that drives not only profit but also meaningful impact. Purpose-driven companies attract loyal customers, motivated employees, and committed investors.

   Example: Patagonia's vision of environmental sustainability has made it a leader in the outdoor apparel industry while fostering deep customer loyalty.

3. **Communicating the Vision:**
   A vision must be communicated effectively to inspire stakeholders. Entrepreneurs should craft a narrative that resonates with their audience, clearly explaining the problem they aim to solve and the value they bring.

Building the Right Team

No entrepreneur can bring a vision to life alone. Success depends on assembling a team that shares the vision and complements the founder's skills.

1. **Identifying Core Team Members:**
   The early stages of a venture require a small, versatile team. Entrepreneurs should seek individuals with diverse skills who can adapt to changing needs. Key roles often include a technical expert, a business strategist, and a

creative thinker.

2. **Fostering a Collaborative Culture:**
   A strong team thrives on collaboration, trust, and shared purpose. Entrepreneurs should prioritize open communication and create an environment where ideas are freely exchanged and challenges are tackled collectively.

3. **Hiring for Growth:**
   As the venture scales, the team must grow. Entrepreneurs should hire strategically, focusing on individuals who bring expertise and align with the company's culture and values.

   Example: Google's early hires were not just talented engineers but also individuals who believed in the company's mission to organize the world's information.

Planning and Execution: From Idea to Prototype

Once the vision is defined and the team is in place, the next step is execution. This involves turning ideas into prototypes, testing concepts, and refining the product or service.

1. **Start with a Minimum Viable Product (MVP):**
   The MVP is a simplified version of the product that addresses the core problem. It allows entrepreneurs to test their ideas with minimal resources and gather feedback for improvement.

   Example: Dropbox began as a simple explainer video, which validated demand for its file-sharing solution before the product was fully developed.

2. **Iterate Based on Feedback:**
   Successful entrepreneurs embrace iteration. They use customer feedback to refine their MVP, addressing pain points and enhancing functionality.

3. **Develop a Go-to-Market Strategy:**
   A clear go-to-market strategy outlines how the product will reach its target audience. This includes identifying the ideal customer, choosing distribution channels, and crafting a compelling value proposition.

Overcoming Challenges

The journey from vision to reality is fraught with challenges, from funding constraints to unexpected setbacks. Resilience and adaptability are essential for navigating these hurdles.

1. **Securing Funding:**
   Entrepreneurs often face financial challenges in the early stages. They must explore various funding options, including bootstrapping, angel investors, venture capital, and crowdfunding.

   Example: Airbnb's founders famously sold cereal boxes during their early days to fund their business while pitching to investors.

2. **Managing Uncertainty:**
   The entrepreneurial journey is unpredictable. Entrepreneurs must be comfortable with ambiguity and ready to pivot when necessary.

   Example: Slack started as an internal communication tool for a gaming company. When the game failed, the founders pivoted to focus on Slack, which became a global success.

3. **Building Credibility:**
   Startups often struggle to gain credibility in competitive markets. Entrepreneurs can overcome this by showcasing expertise, building strong partnerships, and delivering consistent value to customers.

Scaling the Vision

Scaling is one of the most critical phases of bringing a vision to reality. It requires careful planning to ensure that growth is sustainable and aligns with the company's mission.

1. **Expanding the Customer Base:**
   Entrepreneurs should identify new markets and customer segments to grow their business. This may involve tailoring the product or marketing strategies to different audiences.

2. **Streamlining Operations:**
   As demand increases, operational efficiency becomes vital. Entrepreneurs should invest in systems and processes that enable scalability, such as automation and supply chain optimization.

3. **Strengthening the Brand:**
   A strong brand creates trust and loyalty, helping startups stand out in crowded markets. Entrepreneurs should focus on delivering a consistent message and exceptional customer experiences.

   Example: Apple's brand emphasizes simplicity, design, and innovation, making it a global leader in consumer technology.

4. **Maintaining Focus:**
   Rapid growth can lead to mission drift. Entrepreneurs must stay true to their vision and ensure that all decisions align with their long-term goals.

Leveraging Partnerships and Networks

Partnerships can amplify an entrepreneur's efforts, providing access to resources, expertise, and markets.

1. **Strategic Alliances:**
    Collaborating with other companies can help startups overcome resource constraints and scale faster. For example, partnerships with established brands can boost credibility and market reach.

2. **Industry Networks:**
    Participating in industry events and joining networks can provide valuable connections and insights. Entrepreneurs should actively seek opportunities to engage with mentors, investors, and peers.

3. **Community Support:**
    Building a community around the brand fosters loyalty and advocacy. Entrepreneurs can engage their audience through social media, events, and content marketing.

    Example: Tesla's community of enthusiasts has played a key role in promoting its electric vehicles and mission to accelerate sustainable energy.

Measuring Success and Iterating

Success is not a destination; it is an ongoing process. Entrepreneurs must continuously measure their progress and adapt their strategies to achieve their goals.

1. **Key Performance Indicators (KPIs):**
    Clear metrics help entrepreneurs track their performance and identify areas for improvement. Common KPIs include revenue growth, customer acquisition, and user engagement.

2. **Customer Feedback:**
    Listening to customers is essential for staying relevant and competitive. Regular feedback loops help entrepreneurs understand evolving needs and refine their offerings.

3. **Learning from Failure:**
   Setbacks are inevitable, but they provide valuable lessons. Entrepreneurs should analyze failures objectively and use them as opportunities for growth.

   Example: Netflix originally started as a DVD rental service but shifted to streaming after recognizing changing consumer preferences.

The Role of Visionary Leadership

Visionary leaders play a pivotal role in transforming ideas into reality. They inspire their teams, make bold decisions, and navigate uncertainty with confidence.

1. **Inspiring Others:**
   Great leaders articulate their vision in a way that resonates with employees, investors, and customers. They build enthusiasm and foster a sense of shared purpose.

   Example: Steve Jobs' ability to communicate Apple's vision of "thinking differently" inspired both his team and the broader public.

2. **Making Tough Decisions:**
   Leadership often involves difficult choices, from pivoting business models to cutting unviable projects. Visionary leaders prioritize long-term goals over short-term gains.

3. **Fostering Innovation:**
   Leaders must create an environment where creativity and experimentation thrive. Encouraging risk-taking and learning from mistakes is essential for driving innovation.

Case Studies: Vision to Reality

1. **Airbnb:**
   Airbnb started with a simple vision: to connect people who have space with those who need a place to stay. Through relentless iteration, strategic partnerships, and a strong focus on customer experience, Airbnb transformed into a global marketplace for hospitality.

2. **Tesla:**
   Tesla's vision of sustainable energy began with luxury electric cars but expanded to include solar energy and battery storage. By focusing on innovation, branding, and scalability, Tesla disrupted multiple industries.

3. **SpaceX:**
   SpaceX's goal of reducing the cost of space travel required overcoming numerous technical and financial challenges. Through a methodical approach to prototyping, testing, and scaling, the company achieved milestones like reusable rockets and commercial space missions.

Conclusion: The Journey to Realizing a Vision

Turning a vision into reality is a journey marked by creativity, resilience, and perseverance. It requires entrepreneurs to dream big, plan meticulously, and execute with precision. Along the way, they must navigate challenges, build strong teams, and remain true to their mission.

In today's world, the opportunities for innovation are limitless. Entrepreneurs who embrace the process of transformation—who are unafraid to take risks and learn from failure—have the power to shape industries, solve global problems, and leave a lasting legacy.

The journey is not easy, but for those willing to take it, the rewards are immeasurable

Chapter 8: Thriving in the Age of Abundance

Humanity is on the verge of an extraordinary transformation. For the first time in history, advancements in technology, coupled with innovative thinking, have the potential to solve the problems of scarcity that have defined our existence for millennia. Energy, food, healthcare, and education—once limited and inaccessible for billions—are becoming more abundant and equitable through technological breakthroughs and global collaboration. This unprecedented era, often referred to as the *Age of Abundance,* presents both opportunities and challenges for entrepreneurs.

For those who understand the dynamics of this shift, the Age of Abundance is not just a technological or economic phenomenon; it is a call to action. Entrepreneurs have a unique role to play in driving this abundance by leveraging emerging technologies, creating scalable solutions, and addressing systemic inequities. This chapter explores the principles of abundance, the tools and strategies entrepreneurs can use to thrive, and the responsibilities they bear in shaping a future that benefits all.

The Concept of Abundance

Abundance challenges the long-standing notion of scarcity that has governed much of human behavior and economic thought. For centuries, resources were finite, competition was inevitable, and access was limited to those with privilege or wealth. However, technology is rapidly redefining these dynamics:

1. **Energy:**
   Renewable energy sources like solar, wind, and geothermal have made it possible to generate power at unprecedented scales and decreasing costs. Innovations in energy storage and grid management are further democratizing access to electricity.

2. **Food:**
   Precision agriculture, vertical farming, and lab-grown meats are transforming food production. These technologies not only increase yields but also reduce the environmental footprint of traditional farming methods.

3. **Healthcare:**
   AI, biotechnology, and telemedicine are making healthcare more personalized, efficient, and accessible. Vaccines, diagnostics, and treatments that once required years to develop are now being created in record time.

4. **Education:**
   Online learning platforms, open educational resources, and AI-powered tutoring systems are breaking down barriers to education, enabling people around the world to gain skills and knowledge.

In essence, abundance means creating systems that can deliver more—more resources, more opportunities, and more value—to more people. It is about scaling solutions so that they are not limited by geography, class, or circumstance.

The Entrepreneur's Role in the Age of Abundance

Entrepreneurs are uniquely positioned to be the architects of abundance. Their ability to identify opportunities, innovate, and execute at scale makes them essential to addressing the challenges and leveraging the opportunities of this new era.

1. **Innovating Beyond Scarcity:**
   Entrepreneurs must reimagine industries traditionally defined by scarcity. For example, rather than optimizing oil extraction, they can focus on renewable energy technologies that make fossil fuels obsolete.

   Case Study: Tesla redefined the automotive and energy sectors by focusing on scalable, renewable solutions such as electric vehicles and solar energy products.

2. **Scaling Impact:**
   The Age of Abundance requires solutions that are scalable, ensuring they can reach billions of people. Entrepreneurs must prioritize business models that leverage technology to grow efficiently.

   Case Study: Google's mission to "organize the world's information and make it universally accessible and useful" demonstrates how a scalable approach can create global impact.

3. **Addressing Inequality:**
   Abundance is only meaningful if it benefits everyone. Entrepreneurs must design solutions that address systemic inequalities and ensure access for underserved populations.

   Case Study: Zipline's drone delivery service is revolutionizing healthcare logistics by delivering critical medical supplies to remote and underserved communities.

The Tools of Abundance

Entrepreneurs have access to an ever-expanding toolkit of technologies and platforms that enable them to create solutions at scale.

1. **Artificial Intelligence:**
   AI is a cornerstone of abundance. Its ability to analyze massive datasets, optimize processes, and provide personalized experiences makes it indispensable across industries.

   Example: AI-driven precision farming uses real-time data to optimize crop yields, reduce waste, and conserve water.

2. **Blockchain:**
   Blockchain technology ensures transparency, security, and decentralization, making it a powerful tool for building trust and efficiency in systems like supply chains, finance, and governance.

   Example: Ethereum's decentralized platform enables smart contracts that automate complex agreements, reducing costs and inefficiencies.

3. **3D Printing and Manufacturing:**
   Additive manufacturing is transforming production by reducing waste, lowering costs, and enabling customization. This technology is particularly impactful in healthcare and construction.

   Example: 3D-printed prosthetics are making personalized healthcare more affordable and accessible.

4. **IoT and Connectivity:**
   The Internet of Things connects devices, enabling smarter systems for energy management, logistics, and urban planning.

Example: Smart grids use IoT to optimize energy distribution, reducing waste and improving reliability.

5. **Biotechnology:**
   Advances in gene editing, synthetic biology, and bioengineering are opening new frontiers in medicine, agriculture, and environmental science.

   Example: CRISPR technology is being used to create disease-resistant crops and develop groundbreaking medical treatments.

Mindsets for Thriving in the Age of Abundance

To succeed in this transformative era, entrepreneurs must cultivate specific mindsets and approaches:

1. **Abundance Thinking:**
   Entrepreneurs should move beyond zero-sum thinking and embrace the idea that technology can create opportunities for everyone. This mindset encourages collaboration, innovation, and long-term planning.

   Example: Open-source platforms like Linux have demonstrated that shared innovation can drive widespread progress.

2. **Mission-Driven Innovation:**
   Entrepreneurs should focus on solutions that address pressing global challenges. A clear mission not only attracts customers and investors but also motivates teams to work toward a greater purpose.

   Example: The founders of Impossible Foods were driven by the mission to reduce the environmental impact of food production through plant-based alternatives.

3. **Adaptability:**
    The pace of technological change requires entrepreneurs to remain flexible and responsive. Iteration, experimentation, and a willingness to pivot are critical to success.

    Example: Slack started as a gaming company before pivoting to become a leading communication platform.

4. **Collaboration:**
    The Age of Abundance is characterized by interconnectedness. Entrepreneurs must seek partnerships and collaborations to maximize their impact.

    Example: The Human Genome Project was a global collaboration that pooled resources and expertise to achieve groundbreaking discoveries in genetics.

Challenges in the Age of Abundance

While the Age of Abundance offers immense potential, it is not without challenges. Entrepreneurs must navigate these hurdles to create lasting impact.

1. **Access vs. Distribution:**
    Even as technology creates abundance, disparities in access persist. Entrepreneurs must ensure that their solutions reach underserved populations.

    Example: While solar panels are increasingly affordable, installation costs and infrastructure challenges still limit adoption in some regions.

2. **Ethical Concerns:**
    The rapid adoption of technologies like AI and biotechnology raises ethical questions about privacy, fairness, and unintended consequences. Entrepreneurs must prioritize ethical considerations in their designs.

Example: Facial recognition technology has faced criticism for biases that disproportionately affect marginalized communities.

3. **Sustainability:**
   Scaling abundance without considering environmental impact can lead to unintended consequences. Entrepreneurs must prioritize sustainability in their operations and innovations.

   Example: The proliferation of e-waste highlights the need for circular economy solutions in the tech industry.

4. **Navigating Regulation:**
   Emerging technologies often outpace regulatory frameworks, creating uncertainty for entrepreneurs. Proactive engagement with policymakers is essential to fostering innovation-friendly environments.

   Example: Ride-sharing companies like Uber faced significant regulatory challenges as they disrupted traditional transportation models.

Case Studies of Abundance in Action

1. **SolarCity (Now Tesla Energy):**
   By focusing on affordable solar energy solutions, SolarCity has made renewable energy accessible to millions, driving the transition to a sustainable future.

2. **Coursera:**
   This online learning platform democratizes access to education by offering courses from top universities at a fraction of the cost, empowering learners worldwide.

3. **Zipline:**
   Zipline's drone delivery system is solving healthcare

logistics challenges in remote areas, providing life-saving medical supplies and vaccines.

4. **Beyond Meat:**
   By addressing the environmental impact of meat production, Beyond Meat is creating sustainable, plant-based protein alternatives for a growing global population.

5. **SpaceX:**
   SpaceX's innovations in reusable rockets are making space exploration and satellite deployment more affordable, democratizing access to space technologies.

The Future of Abundance

The Age of Abundance is still in its infancy. As technologies continue to evolve and global awareness of pressing challenges grows, the potential for transformative innovation will only expand.

1. **Personalized Solutions:**
   Advances in AI and biotechnology will enable hyper-personalized healthcare, education, and consumer experiences, improving quality of life for billions.

2. **Global Collaboration:**
   The future of abundance will depend on collaboration across borders, industries, and disciplines. Entrepreneurs must embrace a global perspective to address shared challenges.

3. **Circular Economies:**
   Abundance must be sustainable. The rise of circular economies—where resources are reused and recycled—will be critical to ensuring long-term prosperity.

4. **Empowering Local Innovators:**
   As technology becomes more accessible, local entrepreneurs in emerging markets will play a key role in

driving abundance for their communities.

Conclusion: Embracing the Age of Abundance

The Age of Abundance is a transformative moment in human history. It is a time when technological innovation, combined with entrepreneurial vision, can solve the greatest challenges facing humanity.

Chapter 9: The Role of Capital in the Global Tech Ecosystem

Capital has always been the lifeblood of entrepreneurship, fueling the journey from ideas to execution. However, as the global tech ecosystem evolves, the dynamics of capital are shifting. Traditional sources of funding, such as venture capital and private equity, are being complemented—and in some cases disrupted—by new financial models, democratized access to capital, and the rise of decentralized finance (DeFi). Entrepreneurs now have more opportunities than ever to secure the resources they need, but navigating this complex landscape requires strategy, adaptability, and a deep understanding of the forces at play.

This chapter explores the evolving role of capital in the global tech ecosystem, examines emerging trends, and provides entrepreneurs with actionable insights to secure funding, build investor relationships, and scale their ventures sustainably.

The Historical Role of Capital in Entrepreneurship

For centuries, access to capital has been a critical enabler of innovation. During the Industrial Revolution, wealthy patrons and financiers funded the development of groundbreaking technologies such as steam engines and railroads. In the 20th century, venture capital (VC) emerged as a dominant force, financing startups that would go on to define entire industries—Intel, Apple, Microsoft, and later Google and Amazon.

The traditional funding model focused on a few key players:

1. **Angel Investors:**
   Individual investors who provide seed funding in exchange for equity, often taking significant risks to back unproven ideas.

2. **Venture Capital Firms:**
   Institutional investors that specialize in funding startups at various stages of growth, offering mentorship and networks alongside capital.

3. **Banks and Loans:**
   Debt financing has historically been a conservative option, suitable for businesses with predictable cash flows.

While these models fueled significant innovation, they also had limitations. Access to capital was often restricted to entrepreneurs in certain regions or industries, and systemic biases excluded many promising founders.

The Evolving Landscape of Capital

Today, the global tech ecosystem is experiencing a democratization of capital. New funding models and technologies are reshaping the landscape, making it more accessible, inclusive, and diversified.

1. **Crowdfunding:**
   Platforms like Kickstarter, Indiegogo, and GoFundMe have enabled entrepreneurs to raise money directly from the public. This model not only provides funding but also validates market demand.

   Example: Oculus VR raised $2.4 million on Kickstarter

before being acquired by Facebook for $2 billion, showcasing how crowdfunding can launch industry-defining innovations.

2. **Decentralized Finance (DeFi):**
   Blockchain-based DeFi platforms are disrupting traditional financial systems by enabling peer-to-peer transactions without intermediaries. Entrepreneurs can now raise funds through token sales, decentralized lending, and Initial Coin Offerings (ICOs).

   Example: Ethereum's ICO in 2014 raised $18 million, funding the development of the blockchain that powers thousands of decentralized applications.

3. **Equity Crowdfunding:**
   Unlike traditional crowdfunding, equity crowdfunding platforms like Seedrs and Republic allow investors to purchase shares in startups. This model has opened up startup investing to retail investors worldwide.

4. **Corporate Venture Capital (CVC):**
   Large corporations are increasingly funding startups through their own venture arms. This model combines financial support with strategic partnerships.

   Example: Google Ventures (GV) has invested in a wide range of startups, providing both capital and access to Google's resources.

5. **Impact Investing:**
   Investors are increasingly prioritizing social and environmental impact alongside financial returns. Impact funds focus on startups addressing global challenges such as climate change, healthcare, and education.

   Example: The Rise Fund, led by TPG, has invested billions in companies that deliver measurable positive impact while generating strong financial returns.

6. **Government and Institutional Support:**
    Many governments are creating innovation hubs, providing grants, and offering tax incentives to support entrepreneurship. Institutions such as the World Bank and regional development banks are also funding tech initiatives in emerging markets.

    Example: Singapore's Startup SG initiative provides funding, mentorship, and infrastructure to foster innovation.

The Role of Venture Capital in the Modern Ecosystem

Venture capital remains a cornerstone of the tech ecosystem, but its role is evolving.

1. **Globalization of VC:**
    While Silicon Valley has traditionally dominated VC activity, funds are increasingly flowing to other regions, including Southeast Asia, Africa, and Latin America. Emerging markets are now attracting significant attention as hubs of innovation.

    Example: Andela, a Nigerian startup that trains and places software developers, raised $200 million from global investors, including the Chan Zuckerberg Initiative.

2. **Focus on Early-Stage Startups:**
    Seed and pre-seed funding have become more accessible, with specialized VC firms focusing on helping founders get started. This shift addresses the funding gap for early-stage entrepreneurs.

3. **Sector Specialization:**
    VC firms are increasingly specializing in specific industries, such as fintech, biotech, or clean energy, to provide tailored expertise and resources.

    Example: Breakthrough Energy Ventures, led by Bill

Gates, invests exclusively in startups working on sustainable energy solutions.

4. **Diversity and Inclusion:**
   VCs are recognizing the need to address systemic biases and fund diverse founders. Initiatives like All Raise aim to increase the representation of women and minorities in venture funding.

Navigating the Capital Landscape as an Entrepreneur

For entrepreneurs, securing capital is both an art and a science. It requires a clear understanding of funding options, effective communication of the vision, and building strong relationships with investors.

1. **Understanding Funding Stages:**

   - **Seed Stage:** Focused on validating the idea and building a prototype. Sources include angel investors, crowdfunding, and grants.
   - **Series A:** Used to scale operations and refine the business model. Typically funded by VC firms.
   - **Series B and Beyond:** For expanding markets, launching new products, and increasing profitability. Funded by institutional investors and private equity.

2. **Crafting a Compelling Pitch:**
   Entrepreneurs must clearly articulate their vision, demonstrate market potential, and showcase the team's ability to execute. A strong pitch includes:

   - A clear problem statement
   - A scalable solution
   - Market size and growth potential
   - Revenue model and financial projections
   - Traction and milestones achieved

3. **Building Investor Relationships:**
   Securing capital is not just about the pitch; it's about

building trust and rapport with investors. Entrepreneurs should:

- Attend industry events and networking opportunities
- Leverage warm introductions through mutual connections
- Maintain transparency and regular communication with potential investors

4. **Demonstrating Scalability:**
Investors prioritize startups with the potential to grow rapidly and sustainably. Entrepreneurs should highlight how their solution can address large, growing markets.

5. **Aligning with the Right Investors:**
Entrepreneurs should seek investors who align with their values, vision, and long-term goals. The right investors offer more than capital—they provide mentorship, networks, and strategic guidance.

Challenges in Securing Capital

Despite the abundance of funding options, entrepreneurs face several challenges in raising capital:

1. **Geographic Disparities:**
While global funding is increasing, significant disparities remain. Entrepreneurs in emerging markets often face greater challenges in accessing capital.

2. **Bias in Funding:**
Women and minority founders continue to receive a disproportionately small share of venture funding. Addressing these biases requires systemic change and proactive efforts by investors.

Example: In 2020, only 2.3% of VC funding in the U.S. went to female-founded startups.

3. **Economic Uncertainty:**
    Economic downturns and market volatility can reduce the availability of capital, forcing entrepreneurs to adapt their strategies.

4. **Dilution and Control:**
    Raising capital often involves giving up equity and, potentially, control of the business. Entrepreneurs must strike a balance between securing funding and maintaining their vision.

The Future of Capital in the Global Tech Ecosystem

The role of capital will continue to evolve as new technologies, trends, and challenges emerge.

1. **Decentralized and Tokenized Models:**
    Blockchain and DeFi will further democratize access to capital, enabling entrepreneurs to raise funds directly from global communities without intermediaries.

2. **Blended Finance Models:**
    Combining private, public, and philanthropic capital will become more common for funding startups addressing societal challenges.

3. **AI in Investment Decisions:**
    AI will play a greater role in identifying promising startups, analyzing market trends, and optimizing investment portfolios.

4. **Sustainability as a Priority:**
    Investors will increasingly prioritize startups with strong environmental, social, and governance (ESG) metrics, aligning capital flows with global sustainability goals.

5. **Localization of Capital:**
    Regional investment hubs will continue to grow, reducing

dependency on traditional tech centers like Silicon Valley and fostering innovation in diverse geographies.

Conclusion: Capital as a Catalyst for Innovation

Capital is the engine that drives the global tech ecosystem, enabling entrepreneurs to turn bold ideas into transformative solutions. As funding models diversify and technology democratizes access to resources, the opportunities for innovation are greater than ever.

For entrepreneurs, thriving in this evolving landscape requires adaptability, strategic thinking, and a commitment to building meaningful relationships with investors. By aligning their vision with the right sources of capital, they can not only achieve financial success but also create solutions that drive progress and impact on a global scale.

The future of entrepreneurship is bright, and the capital to fuel it is abundant. The challenge lies in leveraging this abundance to create a world that is more equitable, sustainable, and innovative for generations to come.

Chapter 10: The Future of Tech Entrepreneurship

The world is evolving at an unprecedented pace, with technological advancements reshaping industries, societies, and economies in real time. As we stand on the brink of a new era defined by artificial intelligence, biotechnology, quantum computing, renewable energy, and other transformative innovations, tech entrepreneurship is set to play a central role in shaping the future. Entrepreneurs are no longer just business creators; they are problem solvers, visionaries, and architects of the world we will live in tomorrow.

This chapter explores the trends, opportunities, and challenges that will define the future of tech entrepreneurship. It provides a roadmap for entrepreneurs to navigate an increasingly complex landscape, offering insights into how they can harness emerging technologies, adapt to evolving markets, and address global challenges with bold and impactful innovations.

The Evolving Role of Tech Entrepreneurs

Tech entrepreneurs are no longer confined to building apps or creating incremental improvements in existing industries. Their role has expanded dramatically, encompassing:

1. **Driving Systemic Change:**
   Entrepreneurs are tackling fundamental issues such as climate change, healthcare inequality, and food security, creating systemic solutions that improve lives at scale.

   Example: Companies like Impossible Foods and Beyond Meat are revolutionizing the food industry to address environmental and ethical concerns.

2. **Redefining Industries:**
   Emerging technologies are enabling entrepreneurs to disrupt traditional sectors, from finance to transportation, education to manufacturing.

   Example: SpaceX has redefined the aerospace industry by reducing the cost of space exploration and opening up new possibilities for interplanetary missions.

3. **Fostering Inclusivity and Equity:**
   Entrepreneurs are increasingly focused on creating solutions that address social inequities, from increasing access to education to empowering underserved communities.

   Example: Andela trains software developers in Africa and connects them with global opportunities, bridging talent gaps and promoting economic growth.

4. **Collaborating Across Borders:**
   With the rise of global connectivity, entrepreneurs are building multinational teams, serving diverse markets, and fostering international partnerships to scale their impact.

Emerging Trends in Tech Entrepreneurship

The future of tech entrepreneurship will be shaped by several key trends:

1. **The Convergence of Technologies:**
   The intersection of technologies such as AI, blockchain, quantum computing, and biotechnology will create unprecedented opportunities for innovation.

   Example: AI-powered drug discovery platforms like DeepMind's AlphaFold are accelerating breakthroughs in medicine by predicting protein structures with high accuracy.

2. **Decentralized Systems and Web3:**
   The shift from centralized to decentralized systems, powered by blockchain, is redefining how businesses and communities operate. Entrepreneurs are leveraging Web3 to create decentralized applications, smart contracts, and tokenized economies.

   Example: Ethereum's decentralized platform supports thousands of applications, enabling new business models and governance structures.

3. **The Rise of Sustainability:**
   As the world grapples with environmental challenges, sustainability will become a central focus for entrepreneurs. Solutions that promote renewable energy, circular economies, and carbon neutrality will dominate.

   Example: Companies like Climeworks are developing carbon capture technologies to combat climate change.

4. **Hyper-Personalization:**
   Advances in AI and data analytics are enabling businesses to create highly personalized products and services, enhancing customer experiences and engagement.

   Example: Spotify and Netflix use AI-driven algorithms to provide personalized content recommendations, setting a standard for user-centric design.

5. **Global Collaboration and Localization:**
   Entrepreneurs will balance global ambitions with local customization, creating solutions that resonate across cultures while addressing specific regional needs.

   Example: Grab, Southeast Asia's super app, tailors its ride-hailing, food delivery, and financial services to the unique demands of its diverse markets.

Opportunities in the Future of Tech Entrepreneurship

The evolving landscape presents unparalleled opportunities for entrepreneurs to create impact at scale:

1. **Health and Longevity:**
   Breakthroughs in biotechnology, genomics, and AI are transforming healthcare. Entrepreneurs can develop solutions to extend life expectancy, cure diseases, and improve quality of life.

   Example: CRISPR gene-editing technology is paving the way for treatments of genetic disorders and advancements in personalized medicine.

2. **Education and Workforce Development:**
   Online learning platforms, VR/AR technologies, and AI tutors are revolutionizing education. Entrepreneurs can address global skill gaps and prepare the workforce for the jobs of tomorrow.

   Example: Khan Academy provides free, world-class education to millions of learners worldwide.

3. **Energy and Climate Solutions:**
   Renewable energy, energy storage, and climate tech represent vast opportunities for entrepreneurs to combat

environmental crises and transition to a sustainable future.

Example: Tesla's solar energy and battery storage solutions are transforming the global energy landscape.

4. **Space Exploration and Infrastructure:**
   The commercialization of space is opening new frontiers for entrepreneurs, from satellite-based services to asteroid mining and space tourism.

   Example: Blue Origin aims to make space accessible through reusable rockets and long-term settlement infrastructure.

5. **Financial Inclusion:**
   Fintech and decentralized finance (DeFi) are enabling financial services for unbanked and underserved populations, fostering economic growth and empowerment.

   Example: M-Pesa revolutionized mobile payments in Africa, bringing financial services to millions.

Challenges Facing Tech Entrepreneurs

While the future is filled with opportunity, entrepreneurs will also face significant challenges:

1. **Regulatory Complexity:**
   Emerging technologies often outpace regulatory frameworks, creating uncertainty for startups. Entrepreneurs must navigate complex legal environments and advocate for innovation-friendly policies.

2. **Ethical Dilemmas:**
   Technologies like AI, gene editing, and facial recognition raise ethical concerns around privacy, bias, and misuse. Entrepreneurs must embed ethical considerations into their designs and operations.

Example: Controversies surrounding AI bias have highlighted the importance of fairness and accountability in algorithm development.

3. **Resource Scarcity:**
   Scaling operations in a rapidly changing landscape requires access to capital, talent, and infrastructure. Entrepreneurs must strategically allocate resources to sustain growth.

4. **Global Competition:**
   The democratization of innovation has intensified competition. Entrepreneurs must differentiate themselves by delivering unique value and building strong brands.

5. **Balancing Profit and Purpose:**
   As stakeholders increasingly demand purpose-driven businesses, entrepreneurs must align financial goals with social and environmental impact.

Strategies for Thriving in the Future

To navigate the complexities of the future and seize emerging opportunities, entrepreneurs should adopt the following strategies:

1. **Embrace Lifelong Learning:**
   The rapid pace of technological change requires continuous learning. Entrepreneurs must stay informed about emerging trends and adapt their strategies accordingly.

   Example: Elon Musk's diverse ventures in energy, transportation, and space exploration demonstrate his commitment to mastering new domains.

2. **Focus on Collaboration:**
   Entrepreneurs should seek partnerships with governments,

corporations, and NGOs to amplify their impact and gain access to resources and expertise.

Example: Gavi, the Vaccine Alliance, brings together public and private partners to improve global immunization access.

3. **Leverage Data and AI:**
   Data is the backbone of modern innovation. Entrepreneurs must harness AI and analytics to optimize operations, enhance decision-making, and deliver personalized experiences.

4. **Prioritize Scalability:**
   Solutions must be designed with scalability in mind to maximize reach and impact. Entrepreneurs should leverage cloud computing, modular designs, and platform models to grow efficiently.

   Example: Amazon Web Services (AWS) provides startups with scalable infrastructure to support rapid growth.

5. **Integrate Sustainability:**
   Entrepreneurs should align their business models with sustainable practices, ensuring their innovations contribute positively to society and the environment.

Case Studies of Visionary Entrepreneurs

1. **SpaceX (Elon Musk):**
   By reducing the cost of space travel, SpaceX is paving the way for interplanetary colonization and satellite-based global internet access.

2. **Beyond Meat (Ethan Brown):**
   Beyond Meat addresses environmental and ethical concerns by creating plant-based protein alternatives that

appeal to mainstream consumers.

3. **Stripe (Patrick and John Collison):**
   Stripe's payment processing platform empowers businesses of all sizes to participate in the digital economy, simplifying global commerce.

4. **Coursera (Andrew Ng and Daphne Koller):**
   Coursera democratizes access to education, offering courses from top universities to millions of learners worldwide.

5. **Tesla (Elon Musk):**
   Tesla's focus on electric vehicles, renewable energy, and battery storage is driving the transition to a sustainable future.

The Long-Term Vision for Tech Entrepreneurship

The future of tech entrepreneurship extends far beyond individual innovations. It is about creating a world where technology empowers people, solves systemic challenges, and fosters a more inclusive, equitable, and sustainable society.

1. **Human-Centric Innovation:**
   Technology should enhance human capabilities and address fundamental needs, from health and education to economic opportunity and environmental sustainability.

2. **Decentralized and Inclusive Models:**
   The rise of Web3 and blockchain will enable decentralized systems that give individuals greater control and participation in economic and governance processes.

3. **Global Problem Solving:**
   Entrepreneurs will increasingly focus on solving global challenges, leveraging technology to address issues such

as climate change, food security, and access to healthcare.

4. **A Legacy of Impact:**
   The next generation of tech entrepreneurs will leave behind more than just successful businesses; they will create a legacy of progress, equity, and resilience.

Conclusion: The Call to Action for Entrepreneurs

The future of tech entrepreneurship is filled with promise, but it also demands courage, creativity, and responsibility. Entrepreneurs have the tools,

Conclusion: The Call to Action for Entrepreneurs

As we navigate an era of unprecedented change and opportunity, the role of entrepreneurs has never been more critical. Technology is advancing at a breakneck pace, offering tools and platforms that can solve challenges once considered insurmountable. The global economy is more interconnected than ever, creating opportunities for collaboration and innovation across borders. Yet, alongside these possibilities, we face significant challenges: climate change, inequality, resource scarcity, and the ethical dilemmas posed by emerging technologies.

Entrepreneurs stand at the forefront of this transformation. They are not merely business creators but agents of change, visionaries who have the power to shape industries, societies, and the planet's future. The conclusion of this book is not just a summary—it is a rallying cry. It is a call to action for entrepreneurs to rise to the occasion, to embrace their role as problem solvers and innovators, and to create a future that benefits all of humanity.

This essay expands on the themes explored in previous chapters, offering a detailed roadmap for entrepreneurs to navigate their journey and maximize their impact.

The Entrepreneurial Imperative

At the heart of entrepreneurship lies a fundamental question: What problem are you solving? Successful entrepreneurs identify challenges that matter, whether they are creating new markets, disrupting old ones, or addressing global issues. The most impactful ventures are those driven by purpose—a clear understanding of why their work matters and who it serves.

1. **Identifying Meaningful Problems:**
   Entrepreneurs must focus on problems that are urgent, complex, and impactful. The most pressing challenges of our time, such as climate change, healthcare access, and education inequality, demand bold solutions.

   Example: Startups like Zipline, which uses drones to deliver medical supplies to remote areas, demonstrate how solving critical problems can create both financial success and social impact.

2. **Taking Ownership of the Future:**
   Entrepreneurs have the unique ability to shape the future through their innovations. Their work is not just about creating businesses but about building systems, technologies, and cultures that will endure.

   Example: Elon Musk's ventures—Tesla, SpaceX, and SolarCity—are united by a vision of sustainability and interplanetary exploration, tackling long-term challenges that affect humanity's survival.

The Tools for Change

The modern entrepreneur has access to an unparalleled array of tools and resources. These technologies and platforms enable startups to innovate, scale, and compete in ways that were unimaginable even a decade ago.

1. **Leveraging Emerging Technologies:**
   Entrepreneurs must embrace technologies such as AI, blockchain, and renewable energy to create solutions that are scalable, efficient, and transformative.

   Example: DeepMind's use of AI to solve protein-folding problems demonstrates how technology can address critical scientific challenges.

2. **Building Global Networks:**
   The world is more connected than ever. Entrepreneurs can collaborate with talent, partners, and investors across borders to accelerate their impact.

   Example: Remote work platforms like Upwork and global collaboration tools like Slack have enabled entrepreneurs to build diverse, international teams.

3. **Democratizing Access:**
   Crowdfunding platforms, open-source technologies, and decentralized finance (DeFi) are lowering barriers to entry, making it possible for anyone with a vision to bring their ideas to life.

   Example: Kickstarter has funded thousands of projects, validating ideas and connecting entrepreneurs directly with their audiences.

The Entrepreneurial Mindset

While tools and resources are essential, they are not enough. Entrepreneurs must cultivate a mindset that allows them to navigate uncertainty, overcome challenges, and seize opportunities.

1. **Resilience:**
   Entrepreneurship is a journey filled with highs and lows. Resilience—the ability to persevere through setbacks and adapt to change—is one of the most important traits for success.

   Example: Airbnb faced early rejection from investors and struggled to gain traction, but its founders' persistence ultimately transformed it into a global hospitality giant.

2. **Purpose-Driven Leadership:**
   Entrepreneurs must align their vision with a higher purpose, creating businesses that are not only profitable but also meaningful. Purpose-driven leaders inspire teams, attract investors, and build lasting brands.

   Example: Patagonia's commitment to environmental sustainability has earned it a loyal customer base and a reputation as a socially responsible company.

3. **Collaborative Thinking:**
   The challenges of the future are too complex for any one person or organization to solve alone. Entrepreneurs must embrace collaboration, seeking partnerships that amplify their impact.

   Example: The Human Genome Project succeeded because it united scientists, governments, and institutions from around the world.

4. **Adaptability and Agility:**
   The rapid pace of technological and market change requires entrepreneurs to be flexible. They must iterate on their ideas, pivot when necessary, and stay ahead of trends.

   Example: Slack began as a gaming company but pivoted to focus on its internal communication tool, which became its core product.

The Entrepreneur's Responsibility

With great power comes great responsibility. As entrepreneurs gain the ability to shape the future, they must also consider the ethical, social, and environmental implications of their work.

1. **Ethical Innovation:**
   Entrepreneurs must prioritize ethics in their designs and operations, ensuring that their technologies are fair, transparent, and free from bias.

   Example: AI companies are increasingly focusing on building systems that are explainable and equitable, addressing concerns about algorithmic discrimination.

2. **Sustainability:**
   Climate change and resource depletion require urgent action. Entrepreneurs must integrate sustainability into their business models, creating solutions that benefit both people and the planet.

   Example: Solar energy startups like SunPower are driving the transition to renewable energy, reducing dependence on fossil fuels.

3. **Inclusive Growth:**
   Entrepreneurship should not just benefit the privileged few. Entrepreneurs must strive to create solutions that are accessible, affordable, and inclusive.

   Example: Fintech platforms like M-Pesa have brought financial services to underserved populations, fostering economic growth and empowerment.

The Challenges Ahead

The road ahead is not without obstacles. Entrepreneurs must navigate a landscape that is increasingly complex, competitive, and uncertain.

1. **Global Competition:**
   The democratization of innovation has increased competition, making it essential for entrepreneurs to differentiate themselves.

2. **Regulatory Uncertainty:**
   Emerging technologies often outpace regulatory frameworks, creating uncertainty for startups. Entrepreneurs must engage with policymakers and advocate for innovation-friendly environments.

3. **Balancing Profit and Purpose:**
   As stakeholders demand more purpose-driven businesses, entrepreneurs must balance financial success with social and environmental impact.

4. **Technological Disruption:**
   Rapid advancements in technology can render existing solutions obsolete. Entrepreneurs must stay ahead of trends and continuously innovate.

The Call to Action

The future belongs to the bold. Entrepreneurs who embrace the challenges and opportunities of this era have the power to create solutions that redefine industries, improve lives, and shape the world.

1. **Dream Big:**
   Entrepreneurs must think beyond incremental improvements and aim for transformative change. The most successful ventures are those that tackle the biggest challenges.

2. **Act Now:**
    The time to innovate is now. Waiting for the "perfect" moment often means missing the opportunity altogether.

3. **Collaborate and Build Bridges:**
    Entrepreneurs must work across industries, sectors, and borders to amplify their impact. Collaboration is the key to addressing complex, global challenges.

4. **Leave a Legacy:**
    The ultimate goal of entrepreneurship is not just profit but impact. Entrepreneurs have the opportunity to leave a legacy that benefits future generations.

Conclusion: Building a Better Future

Entrepreneurship is more than a career—it is a calling. In a world filled with challenges and opportunities, entrepreneurs have the tools, the vision, and the power to create meaningful change. The future will be shaped by those who dare to dream, who are unafraid to take risks, and who are committed to building a better world.

The journey is not easy, but it is worthwhile. For those willing to rise to the occasion, the rewards are not just financial—they are the satisfaction of knowing that their work has made a difference. The call to action is clear: embrace the challenge, seize the opportunity, and create the future. The world is waiting.

www.ingramcontent.com/pod-product-compliance
Lightning Source LLC
Chambersburg PA
CBHW082252220526
45469CB00009B/2980